# A CUDDLY TOYS COMPANION

**By Kansas Bowling***

**Illustrations by Moi**

**Forward by Tori Pope**

*\*Footnotes by Parker Love Bowling*

www.farwestpress.com
First Edition
ISBN 978-1-7365388-3-8
Printed in the United States of America

This book is dedicated to Terrible Herbst.

*Parents beware...lock up your daughters.*

A warning from the cool, calculated Professor Kansas Bowling, who holds our hand throughout the treacherous and educational journey that is *Cuddly Toys*.

The film, which is the second feature directed by 24-year-old Kansas Bowling, threads absorbing vignettes into a jagged-edged satire that is, by all means, a mondo movie: a forgotten genre of exploitation documentary that may have by now faded, but made a lasting mark in cinema history with its signature element of using both real and scripted scenes of uncomfortable or taboo subjects.

In *Cuddly Toys*, Bowling's revolving door of females serve not only as cautionary tales, but also as thought-provoking subjects. Is rape ever a gift? What could a person possibly do with it? And what lies within that girl who stands behind you at the store? What is she capable of, and what is she capable of handling?

The movie doesn't skirt around the fact that women are under the constant predatory gaze of men—indeed, in this film, women can barely exist without being objects of attack. Sexual assault is the running theme, just as it is in many females' actual lives.

It's violent. There are no less than four rape scenes, as well as murder, suicide, and mental abuse. At least two characters say "thank you" to their rapists.

The film is sprinkled with elements that unquestionably reflect teenage femininity: butterfly eye makeup, pink hair, heart-shaped sunglasses, dirty knee socks, cutoffs, purple boots. There's plenty of diary entries, and pets abound. Everyone seems to be named Jenny. And although the material is pitch-black, the film's palette is a bright, candy-colored daydream. We get poetry blended with brutality, and humor blended with horror.

And don't think for a second that *Cuddly Toys* scrimps on the topic of virginity. We meet a girl who recounts trading hers for cigarettes, and another who auctions hers off for $7,500.

We even get to study parallel cases of two brand-new ex-virgins: one who believed that losing her virginity would bring her true love, and another who just wanted to get it over with. One is mentally unbalanced, the other clear-headed and logical. One begs God for forgiveness, while the other ends up abandoned on Abortion Island in Mexico. And only one of them ends up happy. It's up to you to determine which one.

The dichotomy of innocence versus corruption nips at your heels throughout the entire film, and seems to present itself on an awful lot of clothing. One character wears a t-shirt that brazenly says RAPE while casually strumming a harp—an instrument that is classically demure and feminine. Another wears a shirt that features Audrey Hepburn with a ball gag in her mouth. Yet another wears a shirt showcasing Michelle Tanner with a wall of angry flames behind her. These constant images of "good versus evil" successfully make the brain do some work, and open up a path of thought wherein sinlessness itself is brought into question.

When it comes to victims in *Cuddly Toys*, the doomed are primarily young and female:

A 12-year-old excitedly writes in her diary about a man who pays special attention to her by "pinching her waist" and "tickling her higher and higher."

An anorexic girl wearing roll-up sunglasses describes her anger issues while a hand towel hangs in the background, ominously smeared with blood.

Another girl recites the American Presidents after her assault, still trying to impress her rapist.

Even Professor Kansas Bowling can't escape. By the end of the film, she's disheveled and succumbing to the advances of her (most likely male) classroom skeleton.

All this said, some of the film's victims are actually men. A trio of female revolutionaries kidnap a man and throw him in a shed, while another character describes blackmailing the married men she seduces. "If you want a piece of this," she says, "I'm gonna take a *real* big piece out of you, buddy."

And so the thought begins to materialize: Who *are* the victims here? If you're waiting for the film to give you an answer, too bad. The truth is that, just as in real life, the conclusion is often quite cloudy.

Although *Cuddly Toys* shines a spotlight on the vile nature of our fathers, brothers, and sons and states that "walking down the street in a miniskirt can be a death sentence," the door is not completely closed on the manipulative talents of women. This is an educational film, after all, and no one's wicked side is to be excluded.

Professor Kansas Bowling attempts to get to the bottom of these pressing questions, imploring (or is it challenging?) parents: "Have we taught our daughters that abuse equals love?"

You'd certainly think so after watching *Cuddly Toys*, but the truth is that so often—as the film proclaims—girls are not born wild, but rather *thrust* into the wild; and they're not looking for trouble, but rather they fall into it. As one character earnestly tells the camera, "You can have a lot of fun. You can do really bad things."

The trials and troubles of the average teenage girl may not seem like much compared to more all-consuming problems of the world, but doesn't everything begin with the individual? We all make up the human race—and so one girl's assault should be felt by everyone, somewhere inside of us.

*Cuddly Toys* is not a feminist piece, but rather a think piece—a new mondo film to inform, invite debate, and to appropriately represent the flies that continuously buzz around the female gender. And after 102 minutes of rape, gore, and extreme stories of teenage girl woes, the most shocking statement you'll hear is...

...well, you'll have to watch the film to find that out.

*By Tori Pope*

*Disclaimer: Before we begin, I must warn you that you are at risk of becoming totally lost while reading this if you have not had a fresh* Cuddly Toys *viewing prior. I mention a lot of names and reference many characters, and if I didn't know each of these actors personally, I would probably be lost too. So please watch my film…again. And if you've never seen it at all, please do so before you bother reading this making-of book because otherwise you will likely drown in a sea of confusion. At the time of writing this, I have no plans of distribution—I would inform you how and where to watch it, but since I can't, I will recommend you just figure it out.*

## A Cuddly Toys Companion

[1]If you are reading this book, I am assuming you have seen my film *Cuddly Toys*, so I would like to say thank you for a) watching the film, and b) being interested enough to read a book about it. Making the film has taken up a substantial percentage of my life, since I wrote the script five years ago and it took two years to make from the first day shooting to the final day of color correction. I am sure some people reading this will be curious how I got it made, which I will try to explain properly—but forgive me if you leave this book even more confused about how exactly I was able to make this movie with no money and no crew. It's like my response when people ask me how I make money: I don't even know how to answer besides stating the fact that I am a natural-born hustler through and through, and I've somehow been able to get by. But the film happened thanks to the incredible team I was able to pull together, the grocery stores I shoplifted from to keep me (and therefore the production) afloat, and the eccentric cast I was able to find. They

---

1 Hello. Kansas's sister Parker Love Bowling here. I bore witness to the entire process of making *Cuddly Toys*. I auditioned for the role of my character Sueann when I was fifteen years old and Kansas was conned into thinking Teddy Schwartzman was producing. I remember having sleepovers at Kansas's shitty St. Mortiz bachelor apartment where we'd stay up late talking about her dream of making this movie. She was nineteen at the time and didn't know which one of her scripts she wanted to make next. One night she woke me up after having an epiphany: she had to make this film next as an ode to her teenage years, and the ending credits would roll over her blowing out her 20th birthday candles. Many years later, even though the credits have changed, the sentiment remains the same. This movie has been a part of our lives for the last six years, and it is finally coming to a close—a bittersweet revelation—and though I can't help but feel a little nostalgic and melancholy, it is remarkable how we can always re-visit a capsule of this period of our lives. And since I was there for almost the entirety of the production and was present for the majority of the stories written about here, I will be providing the footnotes to *A Cuddly Toys Companion* and believe me, there is no one better to set the record straight.

delivered performances better than I could have ever imagined, and really made the film what it is by fully being themselves on camera. I will touch on first and foremost with how I began the pre-production process casting the film, and how I did not want to work with career actors/aspiring career actors (for more reasons than one) but with girls who were comfortable enough in their own skin that I could have the camera roll and have their personalities create the characters.

Throughout casting, I incidentally uncovered various muses—two of whom I had act in the film as themselves and talk about their lives. I held auditions at a now defunct casting studio called CAZT in West Hollywood, which was very, you know, *West Hollywood*, and had tons of actress types come in nicely prepared with headshots and résumés. I still have them all, hoarded under my bed like a serial killer. But as suspected, it was the non-actress types that stood out to me and whom I ultimately cast in the majority of the roles. Sixty-nine girls came in to audition that day—which I've always remembered just because—and it took a full eight-hour work day to meet with each of them. I had sent out a few scenes to read from the script, and the majority of actresses came in reading the monologue Charlotte Kemp Muhl eventually reads in the film about losing her virginity outside of a liquor store. That day, Brissa Monique (Angel), Cynda McElvana (Maude), Sophia Ventrone (Mary), Tatiana Tovar (Tina), Lex Gray (Lex), Marion Moseley (Hariett), and a bunch more girls who I would soon cast came in and met with me for the first time—many of who I became very close friends with afterward. Brissa, now my go-to muse for everything, came in and read an Elizabeth Taylor monologue from *Cat on a Hot Tin Roof* and Cynda came in hungover on MDMA and flubbed every line, but was so adorable and charming she was able to work her way through it.

Some girls came in and auditioned and after

getting the part, chickened out and said no (or just didn't say anything at all). Most of the rejections were from parents, but some were from the girls themselves. The most heartbreaking one was from a girl named Chelsea who I originally cast as one of Maude's friends. She was so excited to be in the film, but then I stopped hearing from her. I eventually got a text message from her number saying something along the lines of:

*Hello, this is Chelsea's mother. She is not available to be in your film. Thank you and goodbye.*

I assumed she must have been under eighteen and came in to audition without telling her parents. It reminded me of one of my favorite actresses in the world, Jill Banner, who acted in the film *Spider Baby* when she was sixteen and never told any of her friends or family. I actually reference Jill in *Cuddly Toys* before I introduce the "best case scenario":

*She may be acting as a B film star, acting in films she knows you'll never watch.*

I'm sorry, Chelsea! I will cast you in my next movie when you are granted your freedom!

But one of my favorite auditions was from the (in my mind) *iconic* Michelle Hardy. She came in with a chain attached to her nose from her ear and kept flipping her hair and posing for us all, showing off her trade show modeling skills. She had a perfect valley-girl-mixed-with-Latina accent that embodied Teen-Age. I pictured her doing a really good job playing one of the girls at the club watching Sofe Cote play harp, so I told her I'd be in touch like the Hollywood producer I am.

It was Michelle that kept in touch, though. She would send her boyfriend up two and a half hours from San Diego to drop presents on my doorstep, or she would show me photos of me she had printed out and framed on her wall.

When my friend Dylan Mars Greenberg asked to cast a scene in her movie *Spirit Riser*, I asked Michelle to play a member of a girl gang in it. (By the way, that scene is mostly *Cuddly Toys* girls and will be very fun when it comes out. Dylan was also filming for *Spirit Riser* when we were shooting in Times Square, so there will be a crossover scene in our films!) We filmed all day for *Spirit Riser* at Bronson Canyon in the *Batman* caves. It was a hot day, and we were there for three or four hours. When we were done, we walked to the bottom of the hill and Michelle's boyfriend was sitting in his car. Everyone became very concerned and told Michelle he could have come up the hill with us instead of staying down there. But she laughed and said, "No, I wanted him to sit in the car." Everything about Michelle perfectly embodied the young girl of today, with her equating girl-boss feminism to torturing her boyfriend in a hot car. She is truly demented in the best way—which I am pretty sure she will not take offense to me saying.

I had to take all sorts of breaks from making *Cuddly Toys* for financial reasons. Everything was shot over two years, and it was only whenever I had some spare money, someone had given me money, or I was between working on a music video or acting. So it might have been six months or so down the line before I gave Michelle the call that I wanted her in the film. I of course did not expect her to turn it down because of her very open love for me, but was shocked to hear her respond saying she would not be able to. I asked her why.

"Cause I'm dying," is what she told me.

"What?!"

Then I got the whole story from her.

*I caught my boyfriend cheating on me and it sent my body into a state of shock and it made me stop eating and I can't look into the light now and the doctors are trying to get me to eat but I can't so I'm just going to die. But miss you <3.*

I expressed my concern, told her she wasn't going to die, offered any condolences I could think of, and tried to talk sense into someone who just told me they were practically killing themselves over their first boyfriend. I knew Michelle really wanted to be in the film, but she was telling me she was strictly bedridden (when she wasn't in the hospital), so I told her I would hold off on filming the club scene until she got better. (That particular club scene with the girls talking before the harp performance was just shot in front of a piece of black fabric in my closet, so it was an easy scene to re-schedule.)

Then Michelle asked, in a Make-a-Wish fashion, if she could still be in the film but in her current state. It certainly was something I thought about—a real-life story of a girl torturing herself for love fit very well with the film's subject matter—but wasn't going to ask. So the second she offered to speak about exactly what she was putting herself through, I jumped on it before she could change her mind: "YES!"

My muse uncovered. Michelle. A true performance artist. Someone who goes to drastic lengths for drama, and wants it all to be documented.

Only a couple days later, I arranged with my director of photography, Andres Garzas, to go down to San Diego where Michelle lived. I told Andres that my sister Parker would watch his dog, Hunter, who is a big boxer—but when he brought the dog over, Parker crossed her arms and said no[2], so Andres and I stormed out with the dog in tow while he cursed at her in his heavy Spaniard accent: "Parker is really bitch." A classic Andres line.

We got to Michelle's apartment complex in a part of San Diego that's on the border and practically in Mexico. She greeted us by slyly peeking outside wearing protective goggles. She lived with her parents but was home alone. Though she was the younger sister, her older sister slept in the living room behind curtains while Michelle had her own bedroom; a bedroom whose door read:

*DON'T BOTHER ME*

*DON'T TALK TO ME*

*LEAVE ME ALONE*

*NO ME HABLAN*

*NO ME MOLESTEN*

*DEJEN EMPAZ*

And she had some fake blood smeared all over it for good measure.

Without asking, Andres brought his dog in and Michelle told us, "Um, I like can't have a dog in here, cause like, they have germs and my immune system is failing." Andres replied by saying, "Hunter is good dog so he stays." And that was that. Tough love is

---

2 I had to work that afternoon and was not previously asked to watch Hunter. In fact, it was never even mentioned to me until Andres was standing with his dog in our living room. My refusal to watch Hunter was not a bratty act of defiance as Kansas so lovingly implied, but an impossibility.

good in situations like this. Even if it has the potential of infection. Hunter made it into the film too for a second, in the shot where Michelle leaves her room.

Inside her room there weren't any photos of me— but plenty of her boyfriend, along with caricatures of them drawn together from Disneyland and other couple-themed art. Oh yeah…they were still together. But peeking out from under a few were holes she had punched into the wall. Michelle was 68 pounds at the time but was somehow strong enough to break through the wood and plaster. So incredible.

I interviewed her for the film as she sat in her bathroom. We settled there because it was where her eyes bothered her the least. She was diagnosed with photophobia and the glasses that were prescribed to her made her look like she was in a German techno band.

When we were done filming, Michelle hugged me and told me how excited she was to be in the film. She said she wanted to go to Tijuana with me. How was she supposed to do that, though?

"I'll try and get better and then we can go!"

When she said that, I had an idea: "Michelle, only losers are anorexic."

She immediately agreed with me. I mean, it is the hard truth.

I told her how excited I was to go to Tijuana with her when she got over her anorexia. She made it her goal to expedite her recovery then and there.

The whole ride back, Andres kept lamenting: "So stupid! Someone just need to slap her." Which I basically did verbally. Everyone in her life was catering to her illness and enabling it, which was going to kill her.

I am very happy to say that the moment we stopped filming, Michelle stopped starving herself and is back in the San Diego sun—back to her usual antics of posing at car shows. And she is definitely over her boyfriend, it seems, because I subscribed to her OnlyFans and she's been filming herself having sex with some tatted girl.

Michelle has even tried venturing into filmmaking since then, and was going to make a film called *Photophobic* based on her experiences. She did a bunch of photo shoots for it and made a poster, and I'm very excited to see her start filming. But she might have abandoned it in favor of her other project (which I'm also a huge fan of) where she takes sexy photos of herself inside Denny's and Claim Jumpers. I have been setting goals for her to work towards as well. For some odd reason, Michelle has a crush on B.J. Novak from *The Office*, who happens to love Parker. She says B.J. "makes her wet" and she wants to give him a B.J. I told her that once she gets to 85 pounds, I will introduce her to him. He has no idea who she is and knows nothing about this deal I made, but I'm sure when the time comes and she reaches her goal, he will be happy to assist in curing a sweet young girl of a mental disorder.

Michelle is a regular guest at my house the Charles Mansion now, where she is always welcome to come drive her dad's car up and stay (though she doesn't know how to park and barely knows how to drive) and bless me with her eccentric Michelle-isms—like trying to kiss me on the mouth when I'm not paying attention. I doubt she realizes how brilliant they are. One time Michelle tried to impress me with an offer, since she knows how much I love Las Vegas, of free rooms at the Excalibur because her friend "fucks the

King Arthur there for free rooms". I debated whether or not to tell her those rooms are only $40 and to let her friend know she's selling herself pretty short, but never did. The Excalibur is my favorite hotel in Vegas, and I didn't want to spoil King Arthur's fun. It seemed like he was getting a pretty sweet deal.

Michelle is now about 80 pounds, and even though she eats like shit, she's eating! She's constantly sending me videos of her stuffing her face with Twinkies and counting her scale toward B.J. Not only does she think starving herself is stupid now, her ultimate goal now is to get FAT. From the mouth of Michelle Hardy herself:

*So anorexia fucking sucks. So like if you starve yourself you're fucking stupid. I like hate people who starve themselves and like people who are like, "Oh I only eat, I don't eat after 6 p.m." Like shut the fuck up, you can like eat whenever like the fuck you like. "I don't eat breakfast"—shut the fuck up you can eat like the whole fucking day cause like time doesn't exist like bitch, like EAT. I'm gonna be fat because I love eating and I love food. I love fatty and I love fatty shit.*

She is still plagued with problems from destroying her body for that short while. I recently tried to cast her in a video I was filming in Pahrump, NV where I needed tiny girls to be smushed to death by an overweight man. She was so excited to be cast, but told me she would meet us all there because she need a three-day head start. I was more than puzzled. She explained to me that her stomach is so destroyed that she cannot sit in a car for more than two hours at a time without barfing. So every two hours she needs to pull over, book a hotel, and stay there till the next morning. Leave it to Michelle to come up with the most bizarre reason to be kicked off a video shoot. I'm excited to cast her in something else soon, of course— just something more local to her. Or maybe when her intestinal lining is fully coated in Denny's and Twinkies, she'll be back and ready to roll.

I guess *Cuddly Toys* has already saved a life?

There was one day of shooting where I had my friend Kami Eshai come over and take stills on slide film for the props I would use later in the Professor Bowling scenes. (The slides being the ones of Hariett's autopsy and the girls who ran the sex trafficking ring.) I put out a last-minute casting call for girls to stand mugshot style against my blue wall holding their names written on a piece of paper. My friend Jillian Garcia was one of the girls, but the rest I hadn't met until that day. They were all great and I've kept in touch with a few, but one the girls who showed up that day became another muse of the film: Lo Espinosa!

Lo came in with her braces and burn marks all over her arms from the kitchen she worked in and told everyone about how she was ghostwriting a biography for Zeena LaVey. She finished taking her photo for the film, but I wanted her to stick around because she seemed interesting. I wanted to talk with her more to see if she'd be a good fit in any of the scenes I hadn't shot yet, because it wasn't until then I realized I had zero braces in the film—and diversity is something important to me.

Lo then told us that she lived in her car, but not because she couldn't afford an apartment. It was because she liked the "hobo" lifestyle. She even often had car-mates who would share her car. I knew then that I just had to "Michelle" the situation, and asked if she'd like to talk about living in her car for the movie. We made plans to shoot her scene later on.

Before Lo left, she told me that if I needed any financial help for my film she could get me some money. I said that would be great, because I was sure I was spending the last of my so-called budget on slide film that day.

The next day, Lo texted me that she wanted to stop

by and give me something. She came over that night and handed me an envelope that read "Merry Anti-Christmas". I looked inside and it was full of cash. I thanked her profusely and asked her where it was from.

"It's my money!"

I bluntly inquired, "But aren't you homeless?"

To which she replied, "Exactly! I have no bills! I'm rich!"

It was always in times like those where I didn't know where the next chunk of money would be coming from that someone would miraculously step in to help me get the film finished. I didn't expect it to come from this sweet girl I had just met, though, appearing before me like a reverse hobo *angel*—she was the one giving *me* money. I was so grateful and I still have her Satanic envelope drawing hanging on my wall. And since becoming COVID rich (if you know, you know), I am very happy to say I was able to pay Lo back, right before she shot her first 16mm project.

Lo and her stories are ever-inspiring, and not only was she a muse for *Cuddly Toys*, but will be for all future endeavors. Lo grew up in Chihuahua, Mexico but has lived a hundred lives in her car and the sewers of Las Vegas. She was a real Vegas sewer person at one point. It's so incredible. Or when she went north of Las Vegas and helped a Mennonite kid break free of his cult. And then there are all the other stories I probably shouldn't tell. When Lo, myself, and nine other of our friends went on a road trip and Parker and her boyfriend Alan accidentally got arrested in Utah for stealing a dog[3] (long story), Lo was quick to think of plans to get them out:

*There's a lot of people that owe me favors, and it's time to cash them in.*

A loyal friend and a modern-day cowboy.

A burgeoning special effects artist, Lo just got an effects studio in the Toy District and is my go-to effects girl. The props she has been making are blowing my mind. And of course, she'll be in my next film. Perhaps playing banjo, which she has been picking up lately in true hobo fashion.

Lo has been dealt some rough cards in her time, but her story should inspire every whiny social media brat of today. She's never let any of it stop her, and remains one of the most positive, cheery people I know. She's able to laugh in any situation. I have more faith in her success than most people because I know she can handle anything.

We filmed her scene with Laura Kelsey from the Death Valley Girls playing her car-mate since Lo was currently riding solo. We shot it on half a hundred-foot roll of expired daylight film, and I ended up using <u>almost everything</u> she said in the movie. It had to be

3 Rescuing a dog

a fast shoot because the sun was setting, but it proved invaluable—and along with Michelle's scenes and the beautiful scenes with Lex Gray (the woman talking about blackmailing men in return for Bitcoin), *Cuddly Toys* is a real mondo movie. Which makes it a confusing film to categorize, of course. (I wonder if the success of it would differ if it were listed as a documentary…)

Whenever I'm deep in an obsession—whether it be over a filmmaker or a genre—I usually find myself working with some seminal person relating to that world, because otherwise life would feel pointless. And with mondo on my mind, I connected with Robert Carl Cohen, the director of *Mondo Hollywood*. For those who don't know, mondo movies were a short-lived genre from the 60s and slightly into the 70s that all stemmed from the film *Mondo Cane*—an Italian film that translates to "a dog's world"—that featured documentary and stylized footage about "rites, rituals, and superstitions" and other dark subject matter from around the world. The film was nominated for an Oscar for its score by Riz Ortolani, and it spawned a genre of pseudo-documentaries that were often more exploitive than informative.

*Mondo Hollywood* was made in 1967, and was a Los Angeles slice-of-life film that interviewed people from Sunset Strip kids to Hollywood housekeepers to actresses to politicians of the day. A man who owns a beatnik bookstore in Boulder, CO emailed me wanting me to connect with Robert Carl Cohen because Robert was going to be in Los Angeles from Boulder in the coming days, so I went over to a West Hollywood apartment complex he was managing with my friend Poptart Sprinkle.

I didn't have a specific project in mind to work on or meet about when I met Robert, but I knew I wanted to do something with him. So I asked if I could interview him while Poptart filmed. I am not an interviewer and have never really done anything like that (nor do I have a platform to release anything of the sort), but I thought it could serve for an archival purpose. After all, he was around ninety at the time.

He made the interview incredibly easy by doing most of the talking, and at the end of it told me it's always been his dream to do a sequel to *Mondo Hollywood*. He was thinking of making it a 50-year follow-up called *Son of Mondo Hollywood*.

"I can do it!" I told him, though I knew I was barely deep into *Cuddly Toys* yet. This is a perfect example of how I overwhelm myself with projects because I'm always in a rush to work with all my idols, who are mostly in their golden years. I get incredibly stressed when I come up with an idea for a new movie because the more projects I have on the docket, the less I know I will realistically get to make all of them before I die—yet they are all my babies. I just have to move on knowing some will be stillborn. So it goes.

Before Robert left town, we all went to El Coyote. We ended our meeting without any solid plans, but kept in touch. It wasn't until the next time he was in town—I took Parker and some friends to see him speak at LACMA after a screening of *Mondo Hollywood*—I decided to stop the pussy-footing around. I let him know I meant business about making this sequel for him, and offered my little sister up for the job!

Sometimes there are projects that I care way more about getting made for the sake of culture than I do for making them myself. But Parker Love Bowling is the perfect man for the job and already has a good bulk of *Son of Mondo Hollywood* done, with interviews from Bamboo Ben (the SoCal go-to tiki man) to Ivy Nicholson (the former Warhol superstar who Parker met on the subway) to various eccentric Los Angeles 20-year-olds, or what is left of them. It will be an incredibly important film, obviously.

But the most epic mondo connection did not come until later, during a chance encounter in Fort Collins, CO. If you hadn't previously heard of *Mondo Cane* or *Mondo Hollywood*, it is much more likely you have heard about probably the most notorious of all the mondo movies—one that came much later in the genre, long after the trend faded. I am talking about the iconic film that spawned numerous sequels and scarred countless children for life: *Faces of Death*.

Before I made *Cuddly Toys*, part of my pitch was that it was going to be "*Faces of Death* meets *Bye Bye Birdie*", along with clips to the trailer of *Blood Feast* and the opening to *Single Room Furnished*. (That oddly didn't get me any funding.) But the whole structure of *Cuddly Toys* is a big homage of *Faces of Death*, with a professor character talking to an audience, presenting clips and telling stories. *Faces of Death* had the professor showing real clips of people dying, though about half of the real footage was fake. Some of them are pretty obviously fake, but the real ones are…pretty horrifying. This all tied in with driving the point home about how horrifying the teenage years can be for girls.

I acted in a bunch of movies and short films during the time I was making *Cuddly Toys* to supplement the budget. Most of them were great experiences (with some huge exceptions), and the trip to Fort Collins where the next chance encounter took place was one of my favorite and most memorable. A filmmaker named Laura Conway in Denver reached out to me to act in her short film *Dolphy* on a recommendation from Katie Hinshaw, her awesome cinematographer and curator of the film zine *Analog Cookbook*. After picking me up from the airport, I was telling Laura about *Cuddly Toys* and gave her my *"Faces of Death/Bye Bye Birdie"* pitch, and she stopped me.

*"Faces of Death?* The other actress in *Dolphy* married to the guy who made that movie!"

Mind you, there were only a handful of people in this whole movie. I played a botanist who was in love with my supervisor, played by a very sweet actress named Ena. When I met Ena, I bombarded her with the news that I was going to talk to her ex-husband one way or another. And as fate would have it, we were scheduled to shoot a scene in Fort Collins a couple days later which was right near the ranch he lived on.

████████████ is his name. The original *Faces of Death* film is credited to the fictional Conan LeCilaire (which he later told me was an attempt at a pun—*le killer*), but was actually directed by two men: John Allan Schwartz and ████████████. Schwartz now is very open about the fact that he made such a messed-up piece of art, and he is the one that does Q&As at retrospective screenings while ████████ has created a career for himself producing shows for the Discovery Channel about women criminals.

After filming a scene with a horse in the snow on a freezing day, we retired indoors to hang out with ████. I told him all about *Cuddly Toys* and how inspired by him I was, and he was nothing but supportive about the whole thing when he could have been threatening to sue me over copyright infringement. I told him about Michelle at 68 pounds and his eyes lit up and said, "Oh, please tell me you filmed *that!*" He was so proud when I told him I did.

Someday soon when COVID is calmer, I'm going back up to FoCo to screen *Cuddly Toys* for ████████████ and maybe go show Robert Carl Cohen in Boulder, and then I'll see from the creators themselves if it really deserves the Mondo Movie Seal of Approval. But if anything, this all proves how magical Colorado can be without even having to mention C.W. McCall—maybe even second in place to Nevada. The Makers of Mondo have retired there, and have spiritually assured me I was on the right path. If you're genuine in what you're doing and you're positive and receptive, things like this will fall into place.

New Year's 2018, Parker and I dejectedly took a Greyhound home from Vegas on the 31st because we accidentally traveled up there with a real-life sociopath with a rhyming name who became very necessary to ditch. Since our Vegas plans didn't turn out, we extended an open invitation to our house, the Charles Mansion (we wouldn't respond to anyone creepy) and a girl named Angel O'Connor asked to come over. We had never previously met her, but after that night she asked if she could move in with us from Orange County. We recently had a "room" open (our large walk-in closet we would rent out), so we said sure. The next three months of Angel living with us somehow felt like three years, both in a good and bad way. She was a wild girl who took up a lot of energy, but she brought it all with to her part in the film—the process of helping me get it made.

Angel and Parker are both Aries and instantly became best friends. They started a vlog called *Lil Angel Cake and PLB* where they would do things like cut in line at the popular Silverlake restaurant Sqirl claiming they had a "fast pass" or prank call rich people's kids Parker went to school with whose phone number she still had like, Anwar Hadid[4]. Angel would do things like go to Zebulon, a popular club, and shout out our address, telling everyone we were an after-hours spot.

---

4 The vlog also consisted of footage of Angel barfing outside of Café Figaro in front of the other patrons at 10 a.m. after having too many mimosas at brunch.

I would wake up to our tiny apartment full of bratty hipster kids calling me a square for turning off their music.

Angel has a major role in *Cuddly Toys* as Fay, who gets raped on a picnic and then kills herself. She said she would do the role only if she could pick the guy who got to rape her. And she wanted to be topless because we had just shot Parker's scene and she was topless. They had an ongoing competition about who was prettier and who had a better body.

I wouldn't exactly recommend Angel's method of casting. She could have gotten herself into a pretty scary situation by going to different clubs in Los Angeles and shouting "Who wants to rape me?!" She would ask any guy she found slightly attractive, and every time they would tell her absolutely not. Even the ones trying to be actors. I'm sure these guys would be fine playing any other role in a horror movie where they kill women, but rape being as taboo as it currently is had everyone scared straight. Which explains why the guy who eventually stepped forward to the part, Jance Enslin, was gay. (This was very much to Angel's dismay. Jance's boyfriend was there while we filmed and supervised the whole ordeal.)

Part of Angel's shenanigans was trying to find a sugar daddy, though I don't actually know how serious she was about it because every time the opportunity came close to becoming a reality, she would do something to sabotage it. When she was initially moving in, she told us that an Orange County kid named Mr. Sunday who unexpectedly made a lot of money from Bitcoin was going to pay her rent for her, which he never did. She also said he wanted to fund my movie. He didn't end up doing either, but I met him and thought he was great and he ended up doing a photo shoot with us as a Peeping Tom. But part of the reason why I love Angel so much is that even though she was a headache to live with, she was very generous and was always asking these potential sugar daddies to fund *Cuddly Toys*.

Parker and I always get accosted by random men on social media, which is very helpful when you're trying to raise money for a film. (As in: they usually buy things you are selling. Troma had printed out 250 or so headshots of me for conventions, and I had about 1,000 lobby cards for *B.C. Butcher*, my first feature film, printed at one point. I'd sell them for $25-$30 each. Occasionally I would get a person just wanting to send me money just to support the film for nothing in return, but that was rare. I mainly had to whore out my signature.)

One of the biggest hustles to get the movie made was having people donate in exchange for an executive producer credit. If you've noticed, the executive producer list at the end of the film is very long. Each of those people donated at least the amount it cost to buy one roll of film (around $200), but some donated much more or sent me rolls of film in the mail.

One day a mysterious account on Instagram with no pictures named Jay Tony asked Parker and I to go to dinner with him at the Standard Hotel for $200 each. I think that week we were dressing like beatniks and reading *Howl* on Hollywood Boulevard with a tin can in front of us for tips[5], so we excitedly told him yes and he told us to "look for the old man".

We got there and we were greeted not by an old man, but by a seemingly normal young accountant who told us he just wanted to meet us and was only messing with us about the old man thing. He said he worked a lot and had a lot of money, but didn't have many friends and wanted to support artists like us. We thought he was really funny, and we had a good time at dinner. At the end he gave us each $200 cash and we parted ways.

Later on, Jay Tony kept telling us that who he was really interested in was Angel, who he'd never met but knew of through us. He asked us to set him up with her. Angel was really excited by this. They eventually met up, and he took her on a huge shopping spree and bought her a lot of expensive clothes. When she came home, she told us all about the adventures she had been on with him. She said she was creeped out by him, but had so much fun shopping, so it was all okay. After they went shopping, he took her to his apartment above an Ethopian restaurant on Fairfax that he shared with a lot of young artists who he let live there rent-free because he supported their work.

One of the girls who lived at this apartment introduced herself to Angel, and Jay Tony was showing off the girl's art, saying how impressed by her talent he was. She made custom piñatas, and she told Angel, "If you think that's crazy, you wouldn't believe what my job

---

5 For anyone thinking this an easy way to make a quick buck and wants to give it a go, don't. Hours of sweating in our turtlenecks and berets in the heat only made us six dollars. Although an older man joined our showcase and read with us, which was amusing.

was before. I worked at a *gym.*"

Jay Tony told Angel he was going to throw her a birthday party at the house and made promises of it being the best party she'd ever have.

And then he told Angel that he wanted to give me $10,000 for my movie.

When Angel told me this, I was over the moon. I had made my previous movie *B.C. Butcher* for $12,000 total and only the actual production of the film was only $8,000, so I knew that Jay Tony's donation could get the film fully in the can, man. She said Jay Tony wanted to have dinner with me to discuss this.

Shortly after, I met with Jay Tony at one of his neighboring Ethiopian restaurants. We talked about him giving me the money to make the movie. It sounded too good to be true: he didn't even want a return on it. He just wanted to support me because he believed in the project. All he was asking for was a credit on the film. Throughout the whole dinner, he seemed completely straight, and I trusted this was true.

After dinner, he took me to a hookah bar next door where I tried hookah for the first time[6]. Only once. I couldn't do it. So we just sat there in an empty black-lit room listening to Mediterranean techno. I believe this was the point at which I sent Angel an SOS message about our never-ending late-night meeting—not entirely serious just yet. Nothing weird had happened, but I felt it was starting to.

Jay Tony wanted me to see his loft upstairs, so I went up. I saw the piñatas and different rooms where different artists lived. He showed me each room and each artists' work, so in awe of all of it, which I appreciated. But then he sat down with me to show

6 "…tried hookah." Sweet little Kansas.

me one of the artists' pencil-drawn nudes collection. I

guess to believe that Jay Tony's intentions were pure and
he didn't want anything in exchange for this $10,000
was naïve on my part, but he was pretty convincing at
acting the role of the rich piñata-artist benefactor. He
eventually started telling me how he'd love to see me
pose for one of these drawings and I told him I had to
leave. But not on bad terms. He said he'd still talk to
me about the money.

I got in a car to go home and told Angel everything
that had happened over text. And in true Angel fashion
without thinking a thing through, she decided to call
Jay Tony before I even got home and chewed him out
until I got there.

"Don't worry," she told me. "He won't be talking
to you ever again!"

I looked at my phone and I had a string of texts
from him saying how ungrateful me and my bratty
friends were, and how he wanted nothing to do with
me.

At the time I was pissed off at Angel, but looking
back I love that she did that for me and it's hilarious
that I was ever angry, because I was probably was never
going to see that money in the first place. He obviously
wanted something else and was stringing us along for
his enjoyment. He wasn't as well-intentioned as we
wanted to believe he was.

After Jay Tony, though, Angel was still on her quest
for a sugar daddy. She found an app that connected
money-hungry young women with rich old men, and
found a boy who was our age named Jacob Epstein,
who went by Eppy.

Eppy came over to our house before they went

on their date. He told us he was a movie producer, but after asking him some basic questions (for instance what movies he produced), I found out he was slightly exaggerating his position in the film industry. Angel kept pulling me aside, trying to make up for Jay Tony, saying, "Don't worry, Kansas, I'll get him to fund your movie."

I expressed my doubt that he would be able to do anything of the sort, but my heart swelled for her willingness to whore herself out for my art.

In the living room, I unfairly berated Eppy— more so than I previously had with anyone, I think, because acting nice and naïve only got me so far with our previous money man. I thought some light bullying could be useful with this guy. I kept telling him he wasn't really a real producer, and he kept trying to save face in front of his date. Angel was hushing me from the corner of the room, but also enjoying hearing us argue.

Eventually I got him defensive enough to say, "Of course I'm a real producer! I'll produce your movie!" I pretended like I didn't believe him (well, I actually *didn't* believe him), and that made him want to do it even more.

He told me that he was working for an investor who was currently funding a Johnny Depp film. If I got a package together for *Cuddly Toys*, he told me he would present it to this investor and ask him for funding.

"Yeah right," I told him. But I was still excited. And so was Angel, because she'd gotten someone for me—even if Eppy did later reveal to her that he was on the sugar daddy app as a gag, and he actually wasn't rich.

I got the package together for his rich Australian investor, but of course it didn't pan out, or I would have probably made a totally different movie. I can't remember exactly what we were asking for, but it was something like $750,000. Eppy had to break the news to me one day that instead of funding another film, he had decided to buy a yacht. He profusely apologized.

But Eppy wasn't going to let this situation get in the way of the epic battle we had begun to prove whether he was a real producer or not. He was going to make something happen for me whether I liked it or not.

At that moment in time, the thing I needed more than anything was a computer. I had been editing on a very old Mac desktop computer (that may or may not have been stolen?). I used Final Cut 7 on that computer—which was already very outdated—to edit music videos, which it could just barely handle. It couldn't even handle going online. I had to do any business like that from my phone. And I knew that if that Mac could only compute the 30 minutes of raw footage shot for each music video, there was no way it could handle editing a feature.

And then Eppy delivered. He saved the day by sending me that sweet text saying "Daddy got himself a modeling job", which meant he had enough money to buy me a brand-new laptop. The first time I went to his house, he had a copy of *The Subtle Art of Not Giving A F*ck* by his bedside. I asked him if he read it, and he said he'd read all he needed to: the forward. But Eppy *did* give a fuck! About *Cuddly Toys*! I will love Eppy forever for this, even though now he does the same thing to me that I did to him. I was certain *Cuddly Toys* was going to get into the Slamdance Film Festival because one of the curators saw it and really wanted it in. I told Eppy about it. When the Slamdance lineup came out with *Cuddly Toys* not on it, Eppy texted me to tell me it wasn't listed like I said it would be. Nice one, Eppy. But I am the bigger person and now admit, like I did in the opening credits of my film, that Jacob Epstein (no relation for Jeffrey) is in fact a producer, and I cannot wait to see the rest of the films he helps make happen! He was completely instrumental in *Cuddly Toys* getting made. And this book, too, which I'm writing on the same laptop. I believe there was some deal made where I was supposed to give it back, but it just hasn't happened yet. Let us just pray that Eppy reads past the forward this time—because there's no way in hell I'm telling him how much I appreciate him in person.

While my computer is on somewhat permanent loan, the 16mm camera *Cuddly Toys* was shot on I now have partial ownership in. The movie was shot on an Aaton LTR, which I have shot all of my projects on since getting it. Almost the majority of my work now. And the entire film was shot with one lens, an Angenieux 12-120mm zoom. And none of this would have been possible without the help of my good friend Tim Pronovost.

Before I ever shot a single thing for my film, I asked the Internet if anyone would lend me their 16mm camera for shoot dates. I was mainly interested in an Arriflex, since *B.C. Butcher* was shot on an SRII and it was all I knew. I was expecting some DP in Los Angeles who was down with the *Cuddly Toys* cause to just let me borrow a camera when they weren't using it. But the great gods of social media—social media being a horrible tool that is bringing about the destruction of humanity, dumbing down an entire generation, making them suicidal, and brewing our impending civil war...but one that has the power for so much good when trying to get a film made—blessed me with Tim Pronovost, the lovely bookstore clerk from

Sacramento, CA.

Tim had my beautiful Aaton sitting in his closet. He had bought it years before to shoot a feature, but just hadn't yet. He'd only tested the camera once. He told me I could use it for the film, but would have to lend it back to him if he ever needed it for anything.

I was going up to San Francisco and Petaluma to make a Super 8 music video, and I asked the artist if we could make a Sacramento pit stop to pick up the camera from Tim. The artist said yes, so Tim and I met up at a coffee shop and had a nice five-minute exchange. He offered a place to stay next time we were in Sacramento, so I offered the same for our place in Los Angeles. From then on out, Tim became a fixture on our team. He made regular trips down to Los Angeles to stay with us, and took myself and Parker (and sometimes Angel) on trips to Mexico or to Las Vegas and helped us out with any current endeavor we were involving ourselves in, like political campaign videos for flat-Earthers.

Tim, who also plays one of my groomsmen at the end of *Cuddly Toys*, helped out with various parts of the movie like Sophia Ventrone's scene as Mary, where she's talking to the camera about losing her virginity. Tim held the lights for that scene. I usually do everything in one take to save film and money, but in this case, it was one very long take of Sophia expertly going through the written dialogue and improvising a little. You would never guess from watching it that the lighting in that scene is handheld because of how steady it is.

For a lot of the scenes, I would light them with my lizard lamp. I had lizards on and off around that time. One of them is at the very end of the film on top of Hariett's (Marion Moseley's) dead head. When we were at the end of filming her segment, I was suddenly inspired to put an iguana in the scene. I had earlier seen iguanas being sold at an indoor swap meet (RIP) down the street from where we were filming, at Santa Monica and Vermont for only $25. I took a mental note that an iguana would make a great prop for a scene. Seeing Hariett lying dead and bloody in the bright red and now blood-spattered room seemed like the perfect spot for a bright green lizard. Dylan Mars Greenberg was there while filming, and I ordered her to go down the street to grab me an iguana immediately. I got one shot with the lizard and then we wrapped, but I fell in love with him. I named him Loveland after the lizard monster of Loveland, OH.

The three short days I had with Loveland were blissful. He would go everywhere with me, just sitting on top of my head. I had a leash on him at first, but realized he stayed put without one. But on our third and last day together, we went to Bronson Canyon to shoot a Death Valley Girls music video that Dylan was directing. The second Loveland saw nature, he bolted away and never looked back. (A nice German man saw this happen and ran up a steep hill to try and catch him with all of us shouting for him not to, foreseeing his impending fall. The man tumbled back, right on his head, and then ran off…embarrassed and slightly dizzy[7].) Hopefully Loveland is still living in the Hollywood Hills, but he more than likely became food for a hungry Hollywood coyote.

Loveland was the start of the trio of lizards the Charles Mansion hosted, and because of that we had plenty of lizard lamps which were very useful to light scenes with because of the clamp attached to them. We would swap the heat bulb out for an LED, and it worked as good as a Fresnel.

In the case of Sophia Ventrone's scene, though, we were in her bedroom and there was nothing substantial to clamp the lizard lamp onto. We didn't bring a stand, so we just had Tim hold it. By the end of Sophia's monologue, Tim was in tears from being moved by her acting…which is what he told us, anyways. Later I noticed giant pus-filled blister burns all over his hands and screamed. It was from holding that lamp.

"Tim, why didn't you say something?!" I asked him.

---

7 I believe this is the only instance in which Kansas has under-exaggerated. (It's usually the opposite.) The German man climbed about fifteen feet up a steep cliff and fell backward directly onto his neck and left hand. He was a musician for a living, and was worried he wouldn't be able to play guitar. I'm worried he walked off and died later that day.

"Kansas," he told me, "I would burn my hands off for this film."

Somehow I am so blessed to have the amount of supporters-turned-friends that I have. I wouldn't have been able to accomplish most of the things I have without them. Tim has now granted me permanent partial ownership of our little Aaton. I keep it at my place, but now Tim doesn't live far away from me in Los Angeles, where he works at another bookstore by day and writes his screenplays at night. Someday soon I'll be lending the camera back to him to shoot his first feature, which I'll be very happy to hold lights for.

The list of people that *Cuddly Toys* would have been impossible to make without pretty much reads as the producer list in the opening credits of the film. Mickey Madden, who is in the film as Joe (credited as his other name, Reggie Debris), funded a lot of the film early on and funded post—making him the biggest financial benefactor, which I am so grateful for. We have had a long working relationship now, even before *Cuddly Toys*. The band Collapsing Scenery is a two-piece consisting of Mickey and my now boyfriend of almost three years, Don De Vore. I directed three music videos for CS before *Cuddly Toys*, and then Mickey (and of course Don) got involved in the film as well.

The film is very Collapsing Scenery-heavy. Mickey and Don are both central characters—well, Mickey is more of a character. Don is in multiple scenes, and is credited as the "Omnipresent Male". Don's biggest part is outside of the Fiesta Rancho ice skating rink kidnapping Sadie (Sierra Green). We filmed that in a North Vegas casino where I was followed around like a hawk by security while on the casino floor—but anywhere else on their property, such as the ice skating rink, was fair game. We even had my friend Daniel Trujillo (the auctioneer in the film) take the camera on ice to get some shots. (He is credited with additional photography.) The shots we got outside the casino with Don and Sierra were just as easy to steal. The casino security guard rolled up on us, and we were all prepared to tell him what we usually do when we're about to get accosted for unpermitted filming: "We just found this camera at a thrift store! We don't even know if it works! We're just testing it out!" But in a true kind-hearted libertarian Nevadan fashion, he only rolled up to tell us that the sunset behind us was beautiful, and we better make sure we get a shot of it.

The scene in *Cuddly Toys* where Collapsing Scenery plays was not supposed to be as central as it became. The role of Angel, played by Brissa Monique, was miniscule in the original script. It was originally written that a minor character would be seen at a concert watching a band, kissing one of the band members, and then you would later see her lying on a table in a doctor's office about to get an abortion. All with very little dialogue.

I knew I could either stage a concert or film at an

actual concert that was already planned, so of course I thought to make it a Collapsing Scenery concert. Not only is it my boyfriend's and Mickey's band and they're both in the film, but I am also a huge supporter of their music regardless of any of that. I believe they are making incredibly powerful music, and I would rather die than feature a band in my film that makes music any less important than theirs.

It so happened that the next Collapsing Scenery concert was in Mexico City—so I, unfortunately for Brissa, found the only ticket I could afford to fly her out with us. A full day later than the rest of us and after a day-long layover in Monterey, Brissa met up with us in Roma. Her role went from a minor character to what I consider (along with Cynda McElvana's character Maude) the main character of the film. Almost everything we shot with her was improvised. It was my, Brissa's, and Don's first time in Mexico City, and we were completely inspired.

The Airbnb we were staying at had those dogs in it that are featured in the film. And, just like Angel O'Connor, Brissa really wanted to be topless in the film like Parker, so we filmed her breastfeeding the papier-mâché dogs first. Don made the abortion table just on the kitchen table of our house with the band's scrim they use for projection. Collapsing Scenery's projectionist, Zoe Fitzgerald, played the abortion doctor wearing glasses he stole off the face of Alan Yuch—their roadie and Parker's boyfriend—and quickly assembled the headlamp he wears in the scene.

We also had a screening in Mexico City at my friend Santiago Cendejas's cinema. I showed a bunch of my music videos, and then at the end showed a small preview I had edited together of the clips I had already shot from *Cuddly Toys* to the Joanie Summers song "Johnny Get Angry". (Months later, Santiago came to stay with Don and I in Los Angeles and slept in Angel's former room—the closet. When he was leaving and saying thank you, he said the room was great but it got really hot. We found out the whole time he was there, he was accidentally using that damn lizard heat lamp instead of the overhead light.)

Before the Collapsing Scenery concert, we went to see La Isla de las Muñecas (The Island of the Dolls), which we had just heard about the night before from people attending the screening. Don's Central and South American concert promoter, Jerry L, took us there with his girlfriend Andrea Maldonado, and they both made it into the film as Brissa's relatives who abandon her on the island for getting an abortion. Because of the serendipity of the subject matter, Jerry and Andrea let us know that day she just found out she was pregnant.

The musical interlude with Sasha Belyaeva was written into the script, but the second one with Collapsing Scenery's song "Angkar" was a later addition. Both are scenes that people always tell me to trim down (as if I'm asking for their opinion), but I am a strong believer in musical interludes and refuse to compromise. They are an underutilized tool that, in my opinion, has only ever improved a movie.

Keith Allison as my groom

An outtake of Marion Moseley holding a real human skull.
*Photo by Kami Eshai*

The original owner of the wedding dress I wear at the end of the film. When I bought the dress at an estate sale, it came with this photo.

My beautiful Don De Vore who I couldn't have made
*Cuddly Toys* without.

Marion Moseley and me. My bedroom walls and floor took a long time to clean that night.

Don using his body to stop me from sliding while I filmed Brissa Monique in Mexico City.

I took these photographs right after I wrote the script, and I put them together as a vision board. I invited my friends and girls I waitressed with to pose for them.

In front of the Stratosphere (or…"The Strat") realizing my viewfinder is messed up.

Another indispensable member of my team came from a chance encounter. I had a meeting with a cinematographer for a completely different project who was great and very nice, but for whatever reason never ended up working out (I still might work with him someday). I told him all about *Cuddly Toys*. I had just started at that point, and the task ahead had an incredibly daunting price tag attached to it—mainly due to the telecine costs. Buying the film was expensive, but reasonable. I bought it cheaper than the regular price from a place called Reel Good Film that sold leftover film rolls and short ends from big productions. (A lot of *Cuddly Toys* was shot on leftover film from the Ryan Gosling movie *First Man*.) Same went for the processing: it was only around $90 a roll. (One roll equals eleven minutes of footage.) However, scanning the film from its negative to a digital format is where it gets incredibly expensive, and is what turns most people off about shooting film in the first place. You could, in theory, shoot only reversal film and edit analog—but no matter what, there's a point where you are going to have to scan your film to digital. So you might as well do it right away to save you the headache of editing analog versus digital; the former providing no significant artistic merit anyways. Any edit you can do on the flatbed you can do on your computer and it will look the same. That is, unless you're doing any experimental film scratching or cutting—but there wasn't any of that in *Cuddly Toys* at the time. (The one character I scratched out came much later due to ugliness.)

Back to the cinematographer I was meeting with. He asked me if I knew a man named Thom Kuo. I didn't. He told me that Thom scanned film at a big film house where he would get the dailies in from hundred million-dollar movies and TV shows that were still using film and scan them. From the moment I was connected with Thom, the projected cost for my film was cut in half. It changed everything for me.

Thom is the biggest champion for analog film I've ever met in Los Angeles, and runs a sort of underground railroad for starving artists by scanning their projects during his off hours. For free.

Every time I would shoot a scene—and I rarely would shoot any back to back—I would take a subway to North Hollywood, drop the film off at Spectra Film and Video for processing, return on the subway a few days later to pick it up, then walk two miles to West Hollywood from my house to drop it with the after-hours secretary at Thom's scanning warehouse on the hush, sometimes with donuts. Thom would always have it ready for me the next day, and I'd walk back and get it. I think I've spent more time walking back and forth getting film and dropping it off than I have actually filming *Cuddly Toys*. Even more so when I began getting my film at a Kodak drop-off station in Sun Valley behind the Bob Hope Airport. I don't have a car in Los Angeles, so I would sometimes spend all day on the bus there. I tried riding a scooter there once, but it became really complicated when I had to cross all those train tracks and circle back under bridges. If you've been in the area, you know what I mean. But sometimes my dad would drive all the way from Topanga Canyon just to give me rides to these places, or I'd pull from my favor list of people with cars.

For almost a year, I believe, I never even met Thom. He was an enigma. I would just drop off the film with the secretary and then pick it up. After the longest time we finally did meet, and then Thom eventually came to a screening where I accidentally spelt his name wrong in the opening credits. It is now fixed, but I will always be embarrassed at how disrespectful I was to my film hero. Thom even scans film for my sister now, and Lo too. If it weren't for him, *Cuddly Toys* might have taken a full year longer than the already-arduous two and a half years it took to make. He is a true champion of film and filmmakers, and a very rare person to find in a place like Los Angeles, where it can be hard on people like us if you let it get to you. At least the analog filmmaking community is tight-knit. A lot of these people all seem to know each other, and on the whole support each other. Thom is a shining example of this. He operates on a very pure love for the format, and I'm sure that with his generosity, he's made more projects possible for people than he even realizes.

The tagline for *Cuddly Toys*—"There are 100 actresses in this film. Statistically 2 will die before they turn 30. Who will they be?"—comes from what initially inspired me to make this film. (I should probably mention I completely made up that statistic. I remember being very inspired that Stephen King had made up all of the studies referenced in *Firestarter*. That was the first book I ever connected to. I read it when I was ten and sobbed for an hour straight during rehearsal for a play at school. Everyone came to check on me thinking someone had died, but I just told them I was sad my book was over. And then everyone thought I was a little bitch.) In middle and high school, I abstained from most delinquent behavior that I talk about in the movie, but I watched all my friends go through these things. I was far more interested in trying to watch every single American International release, and plus, I was never invited to cool parties ever. I had friends get put into rehab very young, accidentally kill people while driving drunk, falsely accuse people of rape, and have mental breakdowns. A couple of them died.

Within these 100 actresses that I cast, I really got the full range of personalities. I spent two years shooting, and within those two years I saw some of the girls fall prey to these same things. One girl—my old

roommate—even died before she got to play her part:
the opening and closing credit girl, which my sister
Parker took over for her[8]. Some girls from the movie
have become junkies, started doing porn, tried to kill
themselves…and some have turned their lives around.
Some girls in this movie are the most horrible people
I've ever met in my life. I might even get a restraining
order against one. Another girl had me meet with her
manager, who wanted to sign me to a new agency they
were starting together. But then someone working for
them called me a week later, telling me she was quitting
because she found out the agency was a secret Nazi
cult. They were recruiting only Aryan-looking girls,
and for some reason thought I would be interested.
I haven't talked to her since, and I'm honestly pretty
afraid of her. But considering it was 100 actresses, the
fact that there were only a few bad eggs isn't too rough.
Most of them are wonderful, but odd.

By far the most difficult scene I had to film for
*Cuddly Toys* was the one we shot in Las Vegas with
the character Victoria (Charlotte Sartre) overdosing
and shitting herself. We shot that scene in Las Vegas
because a) it's my favorite place in the world, and b)
Charlotte Sartre a.k.a. Goth Charlotte, lived there. (I
had never met her previously, but was friends with one
of the other actresses in the scene, Violet Paley, who
got her to be in the film.) Wrangling that many actresses
at once with my only crew being Parker and Don would
be difficult in itself, but we encountered some even
bigger roadblocks that night—the first being that my
viewfinder in my camera could not focus, so everything
shot in that scene I was completely guessing with. It
turned out pretty okay. (I usually just guess with the
exposure anyway, which I've gotten pretty good at. I
don't own a light meter, but I use an app on my phone

---

8 Kansas told me she thought I manifested being the opening credit
girl. I'm scared to know what she meant…

whenever I feel like I need to. Andres *does* use a light meter, which is why his cinematography is usually sharper than mine, but my style of tripod-less, underexposed, out-of-focus filming captures more of the documentary look I was going for with most of the scenes. Or really, I just tend to rush myself.)

One of the actresses in that scene I had only met a few days before the shoot. I told her and her boyfriend I was going to be filming in Las Vegas in a few days, and he told me that if I put his girlfriend in the film he could get me free rooms with his player cards. I cast her as an added friend in the scene, and then he sent me links to these "free" rooms that were actually $70—and if you know Las Vegas, you know that's more in the middle-tier price range and not even considered cheap. We ended up staying in North Las Vegas, respectively, and no thanks to him. (I would later find out that he's a notorious scammer, and that didn't surprise me.)

Immediately upon arrival, I knew the day would be interesting since one of the actresses was perving out at Mandalay Bay because she has a mass-shooter fetish. After checking in at the Fiesta Rancho, we met in the parking lot of Bonanza Gift Shop (the world's largest gift store), where we went over our game plan. We were in multiple cars, and I instructed everyone to park in the Stratosphere parking lot and then to meet in front of it. The Stratosphere was right behind us—not an actual drive, but just relocating our base. (Pay attention, filmmakers. This is why it is crucial to rent a van for shoot days like these.)

The car I was in drove over and parked, and we walked to the front of the Stratosphere. (Well, it was actually just a few days before they stopped calling it the Stratosphere. The sign you see in the movie came down just a few days later to be replaced with their new sign reading "The Strat". It's part of this tacky

modernization trend in Las Vegas where they are trying
to de-theme everything and make the hotels look more
techy. Treasure Island is now called "TI" and they don't
do their pirate shows anymore. I think Caesar's Palace
has proven you can be high-end *and* themed, but for
some reason the Excalibur thinks that people want to
stay there and not see medieval décor? But I digress.)
We waited for about thirty minutes, still missing a car
full of actresses. I called them all, with no answer. I
didn't see how it would be possible to take so long to
drive from one parking lot to another next door.

Eventually we saw two of the actresses dragging
our newest cast member (the one whose boyfriend had
promised the free rooms) through the casino doors,
wasted out of her mind. When they dropped her at my
feet—her laughing and feeling sick—they told me that
in the fifteen minutes since we had met in the parking
lot next door, this girl was somehow able to down
half a bottle of vodka in her car undetected, and then
proceed to drive a car full of actresses. They explained
how she drove over sidewalks and down the wrong
way of one way alleys, almost running people over.
Risking these girls' lives was definitely not worth the
false prospect of a free room, but I tried to make the
best of it, hoping it would at least read well on camera.

The wasted girl's defense: "You said you wanted
our characters to act drunk!"

After filming for only an hour, things were getting
too hectic. Violet was getting really annoyed with the
drunk girl breathing her vodka breath right in her face,
because Violet was sober. The situation was starting
to get a little heated, so I suggested we all break to
eat. We went to an Indian restaurant where the drunk
girl immediately went to the bathroom to hurl. I went
in to hold her hair back while she braced herself with
her hands directly inside the toilet bowl. She sat back

down and kept her head resting on the table while everyone ate. When we were all finished, Don took a photo of everyone, and her head popped up just for the picture, then plopped back down again with a thud. We had Sierra Green drive her back to the Fiesta Rancho since we were shooting her ice skating scene the next morning. The rest of the scene fortunately went smoothly.

The next day when we were shooting the ice skating scene, the belt to my camera's magazine broke. There is a tiny rubber band inside the camera magazine from the 70s that has small notches that help move the film along inside the camera. It's small and delicate, and the camera cannot operate properly without it. It's a little thicker than a normal rubber band, but it rots and gets crusty like household ones, and they snap easily. I have three magazines for my camera, but I usually only have one functioning because of these things. When I had taken them to get repaired, I had to get the bands replaced with deadstock, so they were just as unsteady as the original ones. Only recently someone I appreciate very much in Ohio, I believe, 3D printed 1,000 of them—so I got my magazines running with fresh parts. Luckily that day I had a rare spare magazine with me, so I was able to switch the film from one magazine to the other. But this is what created the streaking footage in the arcade shots of Sierra. This happened three times while making the film, and I kept the effect in every time. Don was the one who encouraged me to do this because he loved the look of it so much. The jump-roping scene had a lot of footage that streaked when the magazine band broke, and I kept it in for the entire last jump-rope rhyme. And the last time it broke was when shooting the opening credits with Parker. You can't tell, but the credits are actually comprised of two shooting days because of this issue. The magazine broke, and I didn't have a working backup. Since it was just Parker and we were shooting it in our studio, it wasn't a big deal to re-schedule it. I had to get the camera repaired before finishing the rest of the credit shoot, though.

Earlier during the day of the ice skating scene, Don had taken an Uber to B&C Camera (the only camera store in Las Vegas) to buy a tripod head. The Uber driver turned out to be a Troma fan. In the morning, we had him come by to make a small cameo where he finds Sierra's dead body in front of a Budget Suites. (Vegas people find that shot really funny.)

The ice skating scene I had to re-edit more than any other scene in the film, mostly because of its lack of a storyline. Eventually, I had all the girls (Sierra, Jenny Salguero, Elizabeth Zamets, and Parker) come over to my house. I bought them Del Taco and recorded them talking in my closet. I wanted it to sound like they were having the conversation over lunch. I gave them some talking points, had them improvise lines for a good hour, and then cut parts from their conversation into the scene. (Parker always says the dumbest shit when we do this. During this scene's ADR, she said something along the lines of, "I saw you run off with the skeleton man." We also had her do ADR with a group of people for Harriet's funeral scene. Everyone was talking about how they were such good friends with the deceased girl and couldn't believe she was dead, and then Parker says, "This is such a nice spread," referring to the fictional funeral's food display she was envisioning.) But after the tenth re-edit, I perfected the ice skating scene and it is probably my favorite in the movie. I just can't ever listen to "Lady Bug" by Bumblebee Unlimited again because it triggers a stress reaction in my body; post-traumatic edit disorder.

To begin telling the story of how we got James Landry Hébert to play a rapist in the film, I will have to take a detour and first talk about a music video of mine that he assisted on where he may have considered bestiality. When Parker and I acted in *Once Upon a Time...in Hollywood*, we became friends with James, who played Clem Grogan (the one that Brad Pitt punches). He is a true freak, and the cartoonish bully laugh he has in both my film and Quentin's is genuine. It gets me every time. James was adopted by a Native American family when he was a kid and grew up on a reservation in Louisiana. He likes to tell people that the diner they go to in *Easy Rider* is, in fact, his Mama Blackie's diner. Of all the wannabe tough guy cowboy actors I've met, he's the one genuine one I have found. I also think he is a genius. If he wouldn't do silly things like forget to go to auditions, I think he would be one of the biggest actors in the world. Still, somehow he is working his way into more mainstream films, which is rightfully deserved.

Right after I acted in *Once Upon a Time...in Hollywood*, I directed a music video for Nick Valensi's band CRX. The treatment I wrote for the video was based on Haruki Murakami's novels, and I wanted to get a sheep to represent his *The Wild Sheep Chase*. However, animal wranglers are incredibly expensive, and I only had a budget of $5,000 for the video. If I had gotten a wrangler, it would have been half the budget at least. On Craigslist, I found a listing for a sheep breeding farmer in Fontana that was selling his lambs for $150 a pop. When I told James about my plan to go rescue this sheep from slaughter, he was game to drive me out there to pick it up.

We first waited for James to pick us up at our house. He arrived three hours late because he's a "swamp rat" (his words) who lost track of time in his hot tub. I had to explain to the farmer we were going to be late, and he was so frustrated he said we could not have the sheep anymore. We got into James' car anyway and headed toward farmland, hoping I could secure another sheep from one of their competitors in the time it took to get there. I was able to, by some miracle. James, Parker, and I all squeezed in the front seat of his truck. He had his window slightly down on the driver's side the whole time. For the first hour of driving, Parker or I would ask him a question or respond to something he was saying, and he would ignore us and bring up something else. Parker and I would look at each other and laugh. After an hour of this, James realized he should mention that he can't hear very well out of his right ear because when filming a movie in Canada, he got an ear infection and thought putting a Band-Aid over his ear would do the trick in healing it. With the wind blowing into his left ear while driving, he didn't hear a word we said driving up there.

We got the sheep and named her Clementine. Before taking her home, we made a pit stop at Mt. Baldy and showed Clementine off to the locals. A man at the local lodge who had the patio named after him liked her the most. James became very protective of Clementine and was worried someone would steal her, so we left.

We brought her to our house, the Charles Mansion, where she had trouble walking on the slippery wooden floors. She *baaaah-ed* like crazy, and we couldn't keep her quiet until she ran into our closet and saw herself in the mirror and went silent. We tested her by moving the mirror, and every time she lost sight of her reflection she would become vocal again. From then on, we had to have her surrounded by mirrors at all times to help her pretend she was with other sheep friends. I laid newspaper down on the closet floor to protect the wood from her piss and shit, and opened a drawer and filled it with hay for her. By the next morning, she had eaten all the newspaper and had shit and pissed all over the floor. Luckily, it was only one more day till shooting, and then I could donate her to a farm sanctuary.

When we shot the video, James helped out as our sheep wrangler. It was his dream job and he was ecstatic to have a cowboy credit to his name, as opposed to an acting one. He held the mirrors in place around Clementine while we filmed, and she was perfectly behaved. James asked if his friend could come over to the shoot, and I said sure. Next thing we knew, a cowboy on a white horse came trotting down our driveway and James introduced us to his stuntman friend, Jay T. Naturally, Parker filmed the both of them for her sequel to *Mondo Hollywood*.

Clementine had fulfilled her purpose for the video after that day, and now with a new lease on life, she was set to go to a sanctuary. But James had fallen in love. He decided to keep her instead. He tried keeping her inside his house in Granada Hills, but all six of his roommates opposed the farm animal sharing their already-tight living quarters and pushed her to the backyard. James wouldn't stand to have Clementine sleep in the cold alone, so he began living in his backyard as well, sleeping on the concrete with the sheep. After putting up with this night after night, James eventually decided to surrender her to an animal sanctuary in Santa Clarita, where anyone can go and visit her to this day! James later told us about the love he had for that animal: "It ain't natural, it ain't right…"

Finding people to play rapists in your movie is so much harder than you'd think. Actors will want to play literally anything else. Just not a rapist. James had no qualms with this though, because he is the real deal and not some pussy bitch Central Casting nerd, and saw the project as art. (Although the night before the shoot, he *did* try to drop out—but only to recommend someone else to play the role who he thought would be much better than him. Someone named Acid Cowboy. Later when we were filming, he started talking about Acid Cowboy in a take, which did not make the film, but his persistence with Acid Cowboy made me laugh.) For the scene with his hitchhiking victim, played by Lily Noyes, I had him say to her, "This is my bad ear." Having him say this in a situation with a different girl in his car in a new context made him laugh hysterically—probably because he realized how creeped out Parker and I could have been that night by his comment. (We weren't.)

Working with eccentrics can be difficult, but in the case with James it went smoothly and it was well worth the stories that came with it. (And they never end. Like the time he invited Parker to an intimate birthday dinner party for his friend who Parker never met. James didn't show up, and Parker ended up having dinner with a few strangers.) James has a catchphrase that he drops every time I see him that usually has no relevance to the situation—but since the relevance isn't important to him, it won't be to me either, so I'll use it here to conclude the passage about James Landy Hébert:

*Sermon's in the saloon, y'all!*

In the beginning of the film, I project black and white footage of a girl named Ruthe as I talk about her as a subject of study. When I was planning to shoot this, I knew it could be anybody since it doesn't require actual acting to mimic a home movie, so I decided to hire a stranger someone referred to me named Natasha Rogers. I don't actually even recall being sent a photo of her. I just knew she was up for it and I love gambling, so I told her to come over.

I had my wind-up Bell and Howell loaded with black and white film ready for her arrival. This, along with the slow motion footage of Lily Noyes and Nina Ljeti dancing in slow motion during their concert flashback, is the only footage I shot in the movie on this camera—and the only footage I did not shoot on my Aaton LTR.

My friend Kat was over and of course Parker, and at the time I was babysitting four large dogs from the app Rover. Kat brought over chocolate bars with shrooms in them and asked if we wanted any. I did not have much experience with shrooms. I'd only ever taken enough to effectively microdose, and I guess at the time I thought the microdose experience I had was a trip. I don't have much experience with drugs in general because, as I mentioned, I was not cool in high school. I ate a full chocolate bar. Kat said that it would not hinder my ability to film and would just make me feel giddy. She did not realize how much of a baby I was. I was not concerned though, because all I really needed to do was get enough shots of Natasha doing random things around the house to last throughout the 100-foot roll of film.

By the time Natasha arrived, I was curled up in a ball on the couch because the room was spinning and I suddenly became very aware of how bad my hip was hurting me. (On the way back from our hectic Las Vegas shoot, Parker decided to hip check me in Primm,[9] causing me to fall onto the concrete where I possibly dislocated something.) I told them all I couldn't move and I was sorry, and directed Kat to film the scene for me. The camera was already loaded and it was an auto exposure camera, so I was able to teach her in my state to wind up the camera and hold the record button.

The dogs started shitting on the kitchen floor and I thought it was too funny to clean up, so I'm pretty sure we just left it there while we filmed[10]. We were

9 Though Kansas would never admit it, I was merely retaliating, and we were not yet aware of her brittle celiac bones.
10 I cleaned up the shit. I would never leave dog excrement on the floor of our house—something Kansas has done on multiple occasions. Just ask her about Charlie.

in my bedroom and I was laughing so hard. I thought Natasha was Tiny Tim. And then she kept doing this really bizarre thing where she would bend down and get really close to my face and say in a British accent, "Devon, shut up." We kept asking her what that meant, and she said it was an inside joke. With who? We were so confused. Maybe she explained it, but I do not remember. All the dogs were crawling on top of me and one started humping me. Natasha kept looking at me and saying, "You are fucked up." Next thing I knew, Natasha was grabbing both of my legs and twisting them around each other. She was telling me she was trying to fix my hip. She tried teaching me this method to stretch my legs, and put a pillow between her own legs as an example and told me I had to hump it just like the dog was humping me.

*Devon, shut up!*

By some miracle, we filmed the scene. Well, Kat did. She has an "additional footage by" credit at the end of the film.

Sometime later, Natasha came by for our annual "I Have Nothing to Do on Christmas" party and very sternly said, "I was expecting to come over to participate in a professional shooting environment, and there you were on drugs." Ha…sorry. But at least she kept a good attitude through it all. Besides, it turned out just how I wanted it to. And to this day, I still get a text from her around once a month saying, "Devon, shut up." I still don't know what it means.

Casting kids is always the hardest. The jump-roping girls' scene was really difficult because of this, but I really lucked out with easy-going parents on that shoot. Casting the beauty pageant scene was another story, though. The difference in subject matter had parents being much more skeptical about the project (rightfully so), and it took many phone calls and emails explaining the project for what it is, convincing them their daughters were not going to be exploited, et cetera.

The pageant scene initially called for three different girls—hence the three different categories the in the film—but had to be condensed down to one character when the other two girls dropped out the night before. There was a stage mom/fitness influencer I was speaking with about having her daughter play one of the roles, but she was incredibly hostile every time I spoke with her. The day before the shoot, she informed me, "Oh yeah, we live in San Francisco. So if you want my daughter to be in your movie, you have to book us tickets to Los Angeles right *now*." When I told her that was not possible, she said, "Good! I didn't want her in your movie anyway!" Obviously, I did not work with this heathen woman or her offspring. I dealt with all this while I was on set for Glenn Danzig's movie *Verotika*, which I acted in the night before the pageant scene. We ended up wrapping the *Verotika* shoot at 3 a.m., and the beauty pageant scene was at 5 a.m. I only had enough time to shower the fake blood off me between shoots.

My friend Bonnie Bloomgarden from the Death Valley Girls (who cameos in the beginning of *Cuddly Toys* with her middle school yearbook picture as one of the Professor's "subjects") arranged for me to shoot at the Kibitz Room at Canter's, a bar inside a famous Hollywood deli that her family runs. We had a small shooting window of 5 a.m. to 6 a.m. and a lead actress I had casted the day before.

The pageant judges are Galen Howard, my friend and frequent co-star you can see in the films *Swamp Women Kissing Booth* and *The Bridemaker*, both by director Tori Pope; Rob O'Malley, who I also met on the set of

*Once Upon a Time...in Hollywood* (if you think he looks like Brad Pitt, you're not alone—he makes his living as Pitt's body double); and James Kirkland, who I had play Richard Brautigan in my short *Curiously Young Like A Freshly Dug Grave.* Natasha Halevi, who plays Anaconda in *B.C. Butcher*, was the pageant MC. And our lovely pageant girl was played by Faith Dansby, who performed the role perfectly, especially considering the fact that she learned her lines in the car on her way to set. And her mother was the one of the best sports I've come across in regards to stage parenting, which is enough to drive a director insane.

We got through every line of that scene so fast. The judges were all pros and improvised some really classic dialogue. They were so razor sharp that it was easy to get through. I actually had to tone them down at one point. When it got to 5:45 a.m., someone who worked at the bar came in to shut us down early because they needed to set up for a 6 a.m. bar birthday party. Faith was singing along to "Zsa Zsa", the song Dylan Mars Greenberg leant to the film. Faith was hearing the song for the first time, and I was motioning to her to keep going and ignore the commotion that was all around us while I was simultaneously convincing the woman who was working there to let us wrap up the scene. Faith's character had an acceptance speech written into the script, but it was the only thing we didn't get to. Everything else we were able to complete in around 50 minutes. It was like running a marathon on no sleep, but we made it work somehow.

One of the last things I shot were the Professor Kansas Bowling scenes. I planned for these to come last so I could rework some of the dialogue around things I had shot, knowing I'd change some words depending on what scenes I was ultimately going to add or subtract. My DP Andres was going to be busy on the days I wanted to shoot these scenes, so I entrusted my talented Don to shoot for me. He had never shot 16mm before, which added the perfect touch to the footage. The slight mistakes make it feel more authentic, like you're watching a medical film.

Don and I were both used to such hectic shooting days—having to deal with people and schedules and stealing shots—but because it was just going to be the two of us in our studio, we decided to take two days to practice. We created the set with props found at thrift stores. I bought the lab coat and Parker hand-embroidered "Bowling" onto the pocket. The glasses I found ultimately tied it all together and my friend Alexis Michele did my hair and makeup—one of the only scenes in the entire movie where I had a makeup artist on set.

Don practiced his camera moves the days prior with his Blackmagic Pocket Cinema camera. He nailed the fast zooms and pans I had written into the script. I wrote all my lines on big cue cards to practice with. It was hard to learn them all at the time, which is funny to me now after editing the movie: I can recite every single word every person mutters in the entire film. The dialogue creeps into my nightmares.

The day of, we began shooting at noon and wrapped at 3 a.m. It was the longest shooting day we had during the filming of *Cuddly Toys*. An hour out of that day Don spent stringing up the skeleton for the end monologue so he could puppeteer it in a few shots. My deranged way of speaking at the end of the film where I molest the skeleton prop is actually how I felt. I was so tired and no longer felt like speaking. But in the end, it was so relaxed and not a long day compared to the larger sets.

I cannot imagine I will ever want to make a film with a crew any larger than the ones I am used to.

They either feel like a party, with all my friends around helping out and contributing, or they feel intimate like those scenes Don and I made—which are just as nice. Hopefully on screen you can tell that making this movie was not a job but (should go without saying) a passion.

My relationship with Don started around when I began making *Cuddly Toys*, and the film shoot ended as such a close collaborative project that I cannot imagine having made it without him. Don's touch is all over *Cuddly Toys*—from the music to the cinematography to his multiple appearances in the film, and to all the good he inspired in the artistic choices I made. Not to mention his encouragement throughout the entire process. Without Don, I would not have photographed any of it, and maybe would not have even edited it all. I was by no means an expert editor at that point. But he knew that I was capable, just as I knew he was capable and trusted him with shooting the wraparound scenes in the movie as a first-time cinematographer. What I'm trying to get at here is: I love Don very much, but I will stop right here for the sake of being corny, since this is not the time or book for any of that! Okay, maybe I'll also mention that he is a genius and he's sexy.

There were plenty of scenes I had envisioned or wrote into the script that just did not happen, and some that came out way differently than I thought they would. A very good chunk of actresses I cast bailed on me, usually at the last moment, and sometimes the casting would change everything.

The character of Daisy was a last-minute casting that I was so happy with. Daisy is the character who writes in her diary about her friend's older brother tickling her panties. I had a girl scheduled to play her part who was in her twenties, but had a baby face and could play much younger. It made things so much less complicated not having to deal with stage moms—

especially if I would have had to explain away the pedophilia-related subject matter of the role.

I was in New York to shoot that scene, and went to Dylan Mars Greenberg's house where the actress was supposed to meet us. Then of course, around the time she was supposed to arrive, she tells me she can't make it because she's in a completely different state. But she was *so sorry* and will totally act for me another time! If only I could be so blessed. I shouldn't really panic in moments like this because I make my own schedule here, and that day Dylan was my only crew and I really could have re-scheduled, but I like to keep my scheduling pacts with myself.

*Dylan! We need to find a young girl whose parents would not mind her being in my movie...now!*

Dylan's younger sister Summer Greenberg was already playing the role of Hanna, which we were filming later, so we needed someone else. Dylan is a big fan of Nick Zedd and had previously worked with Nick's ex and muse, Darryl Lavare. Darryl has two daughters, so Dylan called her and asked if they could be in the movie. She said of course, told us to go to her house, and said she wasn't even going to be there.

"Are you sure she's going to be okay with her kids being in this?" I asked Dylan.

Dylan responded, "Have you seen the movies she's acted in?!"

When we got there, I was so happy the original girl flaked because no one could be better than the Lavare girls. Jane Lavare played Daisy and had the most beautiful voice-over voice I'd ever heard. She puts Linda Manz to shame. And to make things even better, Jane's sister Justine appeared in the film too, as herself. In the closing monologue of the film, Jane, Justine, and Summer all sit on Justine's bed while she holds her fursona suit behind a "I <3 Anthrocon" poster. Justine was only thirteen, but a furry. But at the mention of anything sexual relating to it, she would gawk at you: "Ew! That's disgusting!" She just liked dressing up like an animal and hanging out with other people dressed as animals. And she was taken to the cons, and no one ever spoiled it for her by alluding to anything sexual. Some day she'll find out what furries are really all about, but currently it's totally innocent and actually cute in a weird way. It's only dirty if you make it dirty, I guess.

The whole time we were shooting the girls' scene, we had another one of our actors, Wayne, wait in the car. We didn't want him to be around kids. After we finished, we went back to mine and Don's apartment to shoot Wayne's scene with Summer. Wayne, who is credited in the movie as his stage name Jurgen Azazeal Munster, plays Ruben, the older brother of Hanna who mocks her for playing with dolls because she's "a big girl now" who does "big girl things". (Wayne chooses to go by Jurgen because, as he says, "I don't want someone watching this movie in Ohio to know my name. That's so…disgusting.") We luckily got that whole scene with only 50 feet of expired film left in the camera, and I had to record the sound on my phone because the Zoom had died. But it worked and was completely usable.

Wayne was initially in another scene that we "shot" at the Santa Monica Pier. Because Andres, my DP, had never shot with an Aaton before, we decided to film a scene to test the camera. (This was before I really knew how to use it either. I taught myself 16mm cinematography while making this movie by watching Andres work, and eventually I took over shooting the film halfway through. This is why all three of us, Don included, are credited as cinematographers.) Wayne, Dylan, and Amanda Flowers were all in Los Angeles from New York filming scenes for Dylan's movie *Spirit Riser*, so we all went to the Santa Monica Pier at night and I had them act like hoodlums stirring up trouble. Wayne had a lot of pineapples left over from Dylan's shoot earlier, and we filmed him throwing the pineapples into the ocean and doing things like eating stuff off the ground saying, "Look! AIDS berries from the AIDS tree!" and harassing street performers. But then, when Andres and I got around to shooting our next test scene (which was Kenzie Givens as Dr. Marie Anbauen explaining the dangers of estrogen), Andres realized he had never fully clicked the magazine into place—so the entire Santa Monica Pier scene was never filmed. (It also explained how loud the camera was being, which scared me for the rest of the production, but I was very pleased to later find out the Aaton is just as quiet as an SRII.) Kenzie is my friend from high school, and we both wrote the screenplay to *B.C. Butcher* together. While I was doing the very important work of directing our Troma film, Kenzie was off working for NASA. She was just in town for a couple days from Indiana to shoot her Dr. Anbauen scene. Most of her lines she wrote herself because she is very, very smart. And getting back that fresh footage from my new camera looking as sharp and rich as it did, I was more than pleased.

Since we didn't get the footage of my New York crew acting crazy, I decided to get it the next time I was in New York. I was only in town for a week, and we kept having to push the dates back farther and farther because Wayne was in Pensacola (which he calls "Penis Cola") and he kept saying he would be in town the next day. But the next day would come, and he would still be in Florida. It was getting to the point where I was getting very annoyed, though it was very typical behavior of him. He would say he was on his way driving up, and then still be in Florida. Crazy how that can happen.

My last day in town came around, and he said he was getting on a plane at last and would be there in the early evening. When the early evening came around, we stopped hearing from him. Unsure where he was, we waited just for a sign of what to do. At that point, it seemed like it was just going to be cancelled. I really wanted Wayne in the film because even though he's a crackhead, he's a really talented actor and comes up with crazy things to say that a person with a normally functioning brain could never come up with on their own, and I knew it would bring a lot to the film. I told Dylan and Amanda that we would do it another time.

Around midnight, Dylan called me saying that she wanted to film the scene anyway. She said we didn't need Wayne, and she could bring someone else, and Wayne could fit into the movie somewhere else. I said why not, and we headed to Times Square to re-create what we had done on the Santa Monica Pier.

It was *freezing* and very late, if you're ever wondering how to shoot at Times Square and have it look as empty as it does in *Cuddly Toys*. Dylan brought her friend Cindy Colon, who was a delight and great for the movie. Amanda Flowers, who had previously thought the scene was cancelled and had already begun indulging in a completely different sort of scene for the night, dropped what she was doing and showed up on ecstasy. Which was the happiest accident that ever happened, because it really helped Amanda, playing herself, speak truthfully and unabashed. Everything Amanda says to the camera at the end of the film is just her talking, none of it scripted, and I think it's the most powerful scene in the movie. It is undeniable she is a modern-day Karen Black, and now after starring in Lloyd Kaufman's new movie too, she is sure to become a huge cult star.

Dylan basically acted as Wayne in the scene and

came up with the name for her character: Wolf Sword Dice Nu Metal H. We repeated the "AIDS berries" line and even sang a classic Wayne tune:

*When he was born, God said damn. Now he's living in a garbage can. He's got no legs and one small hand—Baked Potato Baby Man!*

This song was apparently based on a time when Wayne saw the "baked potato man" he's describing being held by an old woman getting off a short bus, which he said was the scariest day of his life.

The next day, Wayne told us a fantastical story about how he got to the airport to fly to us, but he was arrested because he looked just like his uncle who was a wanted fugitive with the same name, but he was so sorry he couldn't make it. So all was well. (Before we finally got him to play Ruben, there was actually yet another part Wayne was going to play. At the funeral scene we shot in Los Angeles, he was supposed to fly in to play the preacher. He told me he was in town the night before, but the day of the shoot I found out he wasn't. But he sent me $250 as an apology, so I wasn't mad—and D.C. Douglas stepped up to the part the day of and improvised some real priest talk that I probably couldn't have written as well, considering I've never been to church.)

I initially had planned just one trip to New York where I was going to film with all of the East Coast actresses I wanted in the movie. My mom bought me my plane ticket in exchange for a producer credit. Although Don lived there at the time, we had just started dating—and not knowing that I soon too would be living there part time, I tried to pack as much shooting into this one trip as I could.

There were multiple New York actresses that had sent in tapes who I really wanted in the film, and I figured it would be cheaper to fly there to film with them rather than flying all of them to Los Angeles. Not surprisingly, some of the girls who I had specifically made the trip for dropped out when I got there. Always depend on actors disappointing you, and you won't be disappointed. It's more likely than not to happen, since there is a larger pool of unstable narcissists in this group than of the general population. I got to work with so many wonderful actors on *Cuddly Toys*, but I think it really goes without saying that there are some lunatics in the cast of 125 people. Of course, everything worked out, though. There is an endless supply of actresses, and will be for all of eternity. It was not hard to re-cast, but slightly defeated the initial purpose of the bicoastal shoot.

I flew out with Andres. When we had met about this shoot the week before at a bar, Andres was drunk and said he had *so many friends* in New York he could stay with when we got there. I was planning on staying with Don, who I had only been dating for a month or so. On the plane, I asked Andres where he was staying and he said, "I don't know. Where am I staying?" I then proceeded to strangle him because New York hotels were definitely not in my budget. I had a very minimal amount in my checking account, and the only thing I had to spend money on was a new credit card I had just opened with $1,500 on it. And high interest.

I had to buy Wi-Fi to begin my extensive search of finding the cheapest hotel I could possibly find for him. I was able to find him an Airbnb in Chinatown. I also gave him my new credit card to use for food and emergencies. When we got into the city, we parted ways and we were going to meet in the morning.

Meeting up for our first shoot, Andres looked ragged and distressed, and told me that I needed to find a new place for him to stay. I asked him what happened. He very sternly told me he did not want to talk about it. I was so confused about what could have been so bad that he didn't even want to tell me. Don kept offering to have Andres stay with us at his place, but there wasn't another bed and I was being overly cautious about overstaying my welcome (which is hilarious to think about now. Don and I have all sorts of people staying with us for extended lengths of time on the regular that are way more of a handful than Andres could ever be). I told Don, "No, don't worry about it! It's totally fine! I can handle this."

I booked Andres the cheapest hotel I could find online for that night. After shooting in Manhattan, I handed him the 20-pound camera to take back to his *East New York* hotel while I went to the park with Dylan. I'm not from New York. I didn't know much about it at the time. I did not realize how out of the way East New York was, or what that even meant.

I later got a call from Andres in East New York saying he was not stepping foot inside the hotel. I asked him why because I didn't understand. He kept saying it was "skeetchy" in his thick Spanish accent. (Skeetchy has now become a part of mine and Don's vocabulary. It's what we name all the mice we catch in our house. Skeetchy 1, Skeetchy 2...) I had to stop and scramble to find him another place to stay, and ended up finding him a cheap Airbnb near him, since I knew he was carrying so much heavy stuff.

"Don't worry, Andres! I got you one!"

He said, "It better have a roof this time."

"What?!" I said. Apparently the place he slept the night before didn't have a roof. I don't know how that was possible. It also had bedbugs.

"This one is only a ten-minute walk to you," I said.

Andres walked to his new Airbnb…and the address didn't exist. It was a scam that I just paid for.

"I'm *sorry!*"

I found another room for him all the way back in Manhattan. I had to spend $100 on a cab to get him there because I couldn't make him take the subway again like that. Hopefully this one would be okay. I called the East New York hotel to get a refund, and they hung up on me. My money was quickly draining.

When Andres finally got to his new room, he told me it was fine. I sighed with relief. But then he told me there was a snake in the Airbnb. I got nervous again, but he said it was okay—and I delicately left it at that.

The next morning, Andres met up with us at Don's apartment.

"Dude. I cannot stay in anymore skeetchy Airbnb. They had a snake. And they tried to charge me money to take a picture with it."

I didn't know what that meant at all, but I smiled at Don and asked to take him up on his offer to house my vagabond DP. Then Andres pulled out a bag of wet clothes and told us that after doing his laundry in their washing machine, only then did his host tell him their dryer was broken. So we dried him off and got him settled in the living room on the hardwood floor and he was so grateful to have such a comfortable place to stay.

Unfortunately, the next night would also prove to be some skeetchy sleeping quarters, but I had to suffer along with him. We all had plans to go to Philadelphia on a Megabus with the actress Sideara St. Claire to go to Schoolly D's house. Dylan put me in touch with Schoolly, who plays the president in one of her movies.

(For those of you who don't know, Schoolly D is a legendary artist who some claim invented gansta rap.) Schoolly agreed to be in the movie on one condition, besides his fee to appear: he wanted us to arrive with a chocolate cake. We got off the bus at Reading Terminal Market, got a chocolate cake amongst the Amish, and headed his way.

Schoolly's house was filled with his paintings and art, making it the perfect set. A friend I grew up with, Ava Serene Portman, lived in Red Bank and met us there. We didn't really have a scene written, and the one we improvised and fell into was a pretty obvious R. Kelly situation, with Schoolly living with a bunch of young girls. He was so funny. His friend came over in the middle of the shoot and said:

*This reminds me of my pimping days!*

Before we left, Schoolly wanted to show us his "new lease on life" and made us touch a giant artificial vein he had pumping in his arm under his skin. Then he asked for $20 for using his electricity, though we never plugged anything in. I love him so much.

From there Sideara left, and Ava started to drive us down to Annapolis, MD to shoot the next scene with Sofe Cote. I met Sofe when she blindly came to Costa Rica with me the year before on a recommendation of mutual friends, and we made a movie there directed by Daniel Trujillo called *Primitiva*. Sofe was going to school in Annapolis, and was one of the reasons I wanted to film on the East Coast because no one else could beatnik on the harp quite like her. We snuck into her school's auditorium and filmed her scene on the side of the stage instead of on it, faking an "audience" of just Don and Ava.

Afterward we went to our Annapolis Airbnb. And to my defense, not only was this option cheap, but I also thought it would be really fun for everyone. I also didn't know we would be caught in the middle of a giant storm.

I booked us a stay on a boat in the nearby harbor.

We got to the boat, and I acted how I normally do when I want to keep tensions down: I exclaimed how cute the place was and how excited I was for such a quaint experience! We quickly found out the power did not work, and it also wasn't long after that from feeling how wet the beds were that the boat was not storm proof. Ava and Andres got bunk beds, and of course Andres took the top bunk (where he had a steady torturous drip on his forehead all night). Don and I got the "bedroom" at the bow of the boat where the bed was V-shaped. Our heads touched, but our bodies didn't. It was also *just* skinny enough on either side that we would teeter off the edge occasionally. It was more of a bench than a bed. Mind you, the ceilings were not high enough for any of us to stand either and it was cold. We spent most of the night hanging out at the harbor 7-Eleven.

Andres maxed my credit card out within the first three days of the trip. When I asked him how, he said, "I have no fucking a clue."

I believe that the *Cuddly Toys* scenes that didn't happen were never meant to come into fruition. The ones that ended up in the film are perfectly balanced, and any other additions would have tilted it too far one way or the other. One of the first scenes I wrote for the movie was based around teenage rivalry, and it was a girl-on-girl stadium boxing match. Maybe it was too influenced by *Head*. I wrote the script when I was nineteen—which is pretty much going to be my standard timeline considering how many unmade scripts I have and how long it's going to take me to make each one. (At the time of me writing this, I am twenty-four years old. I started filming *Cuddly Toys* when I was twenty-one. Barf me out. I feel a stabbing pain in my chest when I think about how long that's been, because I feel like I could have been more productive. But hopefully the future will bring more money to make more projects, and much faster—because I have a lot to get done, and a lifetime seems like very little time to make it happen.)

There was also a scene in the original script that might have been too "Stephen King", following the plot of *Apt Pupil.* I wanted a sociopathic girl character in the movie who starts killing animals and then graduates to humans. It seemed much too dramatic for the rest of the movie.

Also, when I put out one of my casting calls, I got a submission from Oksana Grigorieva, Mel Gibson's ex-wife. My dad used to play the tapes she recorded of Mel screaming at her for us in the car on the way to school (tape #3 was his favorite), so I was a fan. I asked Oksana if she wanted to be in the film as herself, but she never responded. She might be *Cuddly Toys*'s one that got away because that had the potential to be excellent.

The ending wedding scene could have gone a million different ways. I basically asked every accessible old man I felt fit the bill to play the groom, but got many rejections. The role was originally going to be played by Sandy Nelson, the legendary drummer and former member of The Ventures. Daniel Trujillo grew up next to him in Boulder City, NV and I had met him with Daniel a few times before. I would tell him gossip about Kim Fowley, and then Sandy would call Bruce Johnston in front of me to give him the dirt. It was always the coolest Nevada scene. Wow. Sandy was originally down for the role, but after thinking it over, he didn't want to embarrass himself. He was famously reclusive, and I was excited to get him to agree at all— but I wasn't shocked when I found out he changed his mind.

I then asked Michael Nesmith, back before I knew him (and then decided *not* to know him), but his "keeper" deleted the email I sent. I dodged a real bullet there.

I also asked Arlo Guthrie and actually got a response from his daughter, but she stopped responding after realizing what the scene entailed. This was after I had already gotten excited about this and had grand visions of marrying Arlo in the actual Alice's Restaurant church. I was set to spend every penny I had as a donation to him and the church he still has running—the only donation I'd ever make to a church. I sent multiple follow-up emails, but my desperation was ultimately ignored.

I had been pen pals with Phil Spector leading up to making the movie. He said he was in love with me (that's a story for another place and another time, maybe in a book of its own) but every time I asked to meet him, he would ignore the question—so I didn't think he'd agree to be in a movie. Rumor is he is very insecure about not being allowed to have his wig in prison, so he doesn't allow any visitors. I also researched rules about filming and prison, and that didn't seem to be a thing I could have feasibly done.

Awhile ago, I wrote a script called *Fairfax High* where the lead girl would go on for the whole movie about how dreamy her teacher was, and then at the end her teacher would be revealed to be Little Richard. *Fairfax High* was not high up on my priority lists of scripts and I knew Little Richard didn't have much longer, so I thought to steal that prime casting idea for the end of *Cuddly Toys* instead. I put out a call to the world asking for Little Richard's contact or some way to get ahold of him. A guy in Las Vegas named Manuel Vee said he had his number and could get me in touch with him, but I had to be there when he called because he didn't want to give Little Richard's number out.

Next time I was in Vegas, I met up with Manuel at the El Cortez, and he showed me his tattoos of pugs and sang a bunch of songs about pugs. And then he dialed up Little Richard and we all gathered around the phone in anticipation. And we got his voicemail.

"Wait," Manuel said. "It's Sunday—he's in church! You screwed up. I can't call him twice."

And that was that for Little Richard. But Manuel actually got me the song at the end of the film, "Young Girl" by Hope Organ, so it worked out for the best. (I wanted to use Paul Watkins's version of the song that was in the movie *Manson* originally, but Manuel was friends with Hope Organ and we worked that out for the film. Again, I think it worked out for the best.)

I wrote to Terry Jacks with no response and no surprise. It seems like he's been out of the spotlight for a while, and it's usually because they like it that way. There's no way I could see Terry responding enthusiastically from his home in Canada willing to travel (or have me travel to him) to play a wheelchair-bound old man with no dialogue in a movie directed by a little girl.

Larry Flynt's people also never got back to me. His golden wheelchair would have been a nice touch.

My friend TexasBob[11] Juarez of the band Television Personalities, who ended up playing the minister at our wedding, was trying to hook me up with Chubby Checker for the role. He brought over his friend who had been Chubby's tour bus driver for years. She was enthusiastic about trying to get Chubby in the film, and TexasBob tried hard to lock him in. But with someone as iconic as Chubby, there are a lot of people to get through to give you the go-ahead—and a lot of them didn't want him to be a part of the movie. (Side note about TexasBob: When he was prepping for his part as the minister, he asked me if I wanted him

---

11 SexyBob

to shave his head for the role, grow out his beard, or be fat or thin. I asked him how he would be able to gain or lose weight in such a short amount of prep time and he said, "I can just take off my backpack!" He then lifted up his shirt to reveal a backwards backpack that he had been wearing under his clothes the entire time I've known him, which gave him the appearance of being much bigger than he actually is. His preferred method of baggage is a kangaroo pouch.)

I had my manager look for good eccentric old men too, and he found me one: David Yow from Jesus Lizard. Though many people I knew were excited about this one, it didn't seem right to me because I would never listen to that kind of music.

And then I asked my great friend Mad Mike Hughes, the famed flat-Earther and self-taught rocket scientist. (The story about my relationship with him is also for another time, and also could be a book of its own. So I won't get into that right now.) I think Mad Mike was…*mad*…at me for not being his girlfriend around that time, so he declined.

But then a rush of inspiration hit and I thought to ask an old friend of mine: Keith Allison. I had hung out with him one night years back, and I would always see him at Monkees concerts. Keith was a member of Paul Revere and the Raiders and wrote the song "Auntie's Municipal Court" for the Monkees, but was most popular in the teen magazines of his day for looking like Paul McCartney. And I got him! A very happy ending.

Keith was so brilliant. When he showed up, we all inquired if he understood the context of the scene— knowing he did, but just wanting to make sure.

He said, "Sure! It's about a bunch of girls 'Me Too'ed out of their minds!"

He messed up his hair and stayed in his zoned-out Alzheimer's character for the duration of filming, and kept his perfect glassy-eyed stare in the last shot while I spoke to the camera without me even having to ask him to.

We did the kiss take three times while Don hid around the corner. After each take, Parker would say, "I think you should do another," while Don would audibly sigh[12]. Parker's Lilith is in Scorpio and she's a double Aries, and she's proud of it.

Not only is the wedding scene the last one of the film; it also happened to be the last one we shot because I was waiting during the rest of the production for the perfect groom to come to me—and the world definitely provided. When we finally wrapped, Keith sent me the sweetest message. It read:

---

12 The final kiss that made it into the film was the second take. It was objectively better. My suggesting another take was not an act of deviousness, but me actually trying to help—and I was right, so you're welcome, Kansas…and you're welcome, Keith.

*Kansas, my girl. I had a great time today meeting all of your friends and colleagues. It's wonderful seeing young artisans*

*support each other with their projects. Well, it's official now. I'm a character actor. I never again have to worry about being a former teen idol. A huge burden has been lifted from my shoulders and I am forever grateful. Tell Parker her eyes are beautiful. Can't wait to see the finished product. My love to all of you. Keith.*

As I mentioned before, I wrote this film when I was nineteen as an ode to my teenage years with a welcomed farewell. At that point in my life, my teenage-dom was so jammed down my throat in every conversation I had, every aspect of my life, that I was very happy to be turning a new page in my perceived life—my age had nothing to do with me, but with how people saw me. But at the same time, I was also sad to be leaving a chapter that is so universally romanticized. I vowed to make the most of my teenage years because of it, which I think I accomplished. Making a movie when you're seventeen has people constantly referring to you as a teenager, even when you have far surpassed it. I wrote *B.C. Butcher*, a poorly-made slasher film, when I was fifteen years old and in high school, but I didn't make it until I was seventeen (on the cusp of eighteen). It didn't come out through Troma until I was nineteen, almost twenty.

Yet I was constantly referred to as either a fifteen year-old or seventeen-year-old filmmaker at the time—so people who were aware of that film when it came out are usually shocked to learn that I am currently twenty-four, since the film came out basically yesterday. But a segue into my original point is that it granted me the gift of being an eternal teenager, similar to if I had won a Miss Teen pageant, where you can grow older but you keep your title forever.

I am so happy to grow older because as time goes

on, I am disgusted by everything I have ever written or made prior to that point and time, and I think that symbolizes growth. I am disgusted to have to write a book about a film that I feel does not even represent me any longer, but it is a necessary task in my mind, where I needed to get these stories off my chest so I never have to retell them. Currently, all I care about is living with my sweet boyfriend Don De Vore in rural Nevada and working on our mining claim and listening to C.W. McCall. I did not write a word of this book in the state of California, but split my writing time between the Luxor in Las Vegas and the Terrible's Roadhouse in Searchlight. There is not a single thing I can pinpoint in *Cuddly Toys* that isn't me any longer, but I know it hurts to watch, so I refrain from doing so because it just *feels* so unlike me. Please do not get me wrong: I am very proud of my work, but this goes for everything I have ever made. It embarrasses me to have done it, even though I know it would have been impossible for me not to. And just because I'm proud of something does not mean I ever have to watch it again. It is simply the way of the world.

I will be happy to re-introduce myself to you all in the near future as a CB-radioing prospector, and after that, my *next* incarnation—whatever that may be. But I am sorry to say my *Cuddly Toys* life ended with its final edit and I am never listening to the Monkees again. Like Keith, my teen idol burden has been lifted. Alas, I hope the film takes on a life of its own, curing dumbasses of their eating disorders and saving former teen idols I love from their past selves. With all the empathy in my heart extended to every teenage girl picnicking in the Hollywood Hills, every Catholic girl getting abortions in Mexico, every old Sunset Strip man—I hope you are able to re-invent yourself at whim, because there are so many lives to be lived within your own, and the world is so much larger than the problems we create for ourselves. I'm sure people will leave *Cuddly Toys* with their own interpretations, which I was hoping to do, so I do not want to force my own meaning onto the viewer. But if I could share one message straightforward to my audience, I would say this: you don't have it as bad as you think you do, and this will become clear to you once your experiences broaden. The horrors aside, there are much worse things to be in this world than a teenage girl in America[13].

---

13 I will forever be proud to be a part of this project, and am very proud of my sister.

## About The Author

Kansas Bowling is a writer and filmmaker from California who spends most of her time in Nevada. Her second feature film Cuddly Toys will officially come out later this year, but maybe it has already unofficially come out. When she is not writing or working on films, Kansas is busy prospecting at her desert lode mine and being a custodian of the Mojave Desert. She is also the #1 fan of C.W. McCall.

## About The Illustrator

MOI is the stage name of illustrator and cartoonist Moisés Ramírez Alonso. His work has appeared in TOTEM de Selecciones Ilustradas, Warren Publishing's horror comics magazines, El Juveves, Diario Córdoba, Diario XXI century, and more. He has won more than a dozen awards for caricature and has been exhibited internationally on more than 100 occasions.

# Also Out On Far West

farwestpress.com